The Choice of a Partner

DOES GOD CARE IF YOU MARRY A NON-CHRISTIAN?

DEREK PRINCE

THE CHOICE OF A PARTNER

All Scripture references are taken from The Holy Bible, New King James Version © 1979, 1980, 1982 by Thomas Nelson, Inc. Nashville, Tennessee.

ISBN 978-1-892283-28-3

Printed in the United States of America.

DEREK PRINCE MINISTRIES
P.O. BOX 19501
CHARLOTTE, NC 28219
WWW.DEREKPRINCE.ORG

The Choice of a Partner

There are three choices of very great importance which usually face young people as they grow up: the choice of a Savior, the choice of a work in life (a career), and the choice of a partner in life (a wife or a husband). If we have chosen Christ as our Savior, we should ask Him to guide us in the other two choices; and these other two choices are closely connected with each other, because husband and wife should be partners (workers together) in life. (Read Genesis 2:18–25.)

A Christian should **always choose a Christian partner**. "Can two walk together, unless they are agreed?" (Amos 3:3). "Do not be unequally yoked together [in marriage] with unbelievers"—that is, a Christian marrying someone who is not a Christian. (Read carefully 2 Corinthians 6:14–18.)

You may ask: "How can I know that the person whom I intend to marry is a Christian?" Well, here are some of the things that you should look for in that person:

1. Does he or she witness with assurance that he or she is **born again** of the Spirit of God?
2. Does he or she **regularly read the Bible** and know what it teaches?
3. Does he or she **regularly attend a church** where the Word of God is preached?
4. Does he or she like to **talk about spiritual things**? "Out of the abundance of the heart the mouth speaks" (Matthew 12:34).
5. Does he or she lead a **clean, pure life**?
6. Does he or she have a real desire to **lead others to the Lord** and to see them saved?
7. Has he or she received **the baptism of the Holy Spirit**?

If the answer to several of these questions is no, then you are **not** choosing the right partner.

If you are a Spirit-filled Christian and you marry someone who is not a real believer and so cannot share your spiritual experiences, two things are sure to happen:

1. You will have much sorrow and pain in your own heart.
2. You will not be able to serve the Lord as well as you would if you had married a real believer.

Perhaps you are thinking: "I will marry an unsaved person, and then I will persuade that person to become a Christian." But that is foolishness! Above all else, a Christian is a person who obeys God. So you are planning to disobey God (by marrying an unbeliever) in order to persuade that unbeliever to obey God (by becoming a Christian). You will try to persuade that person to obey God when you yourself are disobeying God! How will that ever work?

A young lady once took a young man to see her pastor and said: "This is the young man whom I am going to marry."

"Is he a Christian?" asked the pastor.

"Not yet," said the young lady, "but I will help him to become one after we are married."

"Before you finally make up your mind, I would like you to do something for me," said the pastor. He pointed to a table in the room and said, "Just climb up unto that table and stand there for a moment." The young lady did so.

"Now," said the pastor, "give the young man your hand, and try to lift him up onto the table beside you." Then he turned to the young man and said, "Now you try to pull the young lady down to you." Within a few moments, the young lady was down on the floor beside the young man!

"That's how it will be when you are married," said the pastor. "You will not be able to pull him up to your level, but he will pull you down to his!"

So it is when a Christian marries an unbeliever. It is always easier for the unsaved partner to make the Christian a backslider than for the saved partner to make the unbeliever a Christian.

Finally, here are three things to remember:

Remember that marriage does not change a person's character. If a person has a bad character before marriage, that person will still have a bad character after marriage.

Remember that marriage is for life. If you buy a bad shirt or a bad dress, it will wear out and you can buy another. But if you marry a bad man or woman, you cannot change that person, but you will have to live with that person for the rest of your life.

Remember that when you have strong feelings about a person or a thing, it is not easy to find out the will of God about that person or thing. Therefore, before your feelings become too strong for you, you should earnestly pray to the Lord: "Savior, choose my partner in life for me. Not my will, but thine, be done."

May God bless you, my dear young Christian friend, and may He so guide you in your choice that you may make the best of your life in this world, and may you reach heaven safely at the end.

Background
of the Author

Derek Prince (1915–2003) was born in India of British parents. Educated as a scholar of Greek and Latin at Eton College and Cambridge University, England, he held a Fellowship in Ancient and Modern Philosophy at King's College. He also studied several modern languages, including Hebrew and Aramaic, at Cambridge University and the Hebrew University in Jerusalem.

While serving with the British army in World War II, he began to study the Bible and experienced a life-changing encounter with Jesus Christ. Out of this encounter he formed two conclusions: first, that Jesus Christ is alive; second, that the Bible is a true, relevant, up-to-date book. These conclusions altered the whole course of his life, which he then devoted to studying and teaching the Bible.

Derek's main gift of explaining the Bible and its teaching in a clear and simple way has helped build a foundation of faith in millions of lives. His non-denominational, non-sectarian approach has made his teaching equally relevant and helpful to people from all racial and religious backgrounds.

He is the author of over 50 books, 600 audio and 100 video teachings, many of which have been translated and published in more than 100 languages. His daily radio broadcast is translated into Arabic, Bahasa (Indonesian), Chinese (Amoy, Cantonese, Mandarin, Shanghaiese, Swatow), Croatian, German, Malagasy, Mongolian, Russian, Samoan, Spanish and Tongan. The radio program continues to touch lives around the world.

Derek Prince Ministries persists in reaching out to believers in over 140 countries with Derek's teachings, fulfilling the mandate to keep on "until Jesus returns." This is effected through the outreaches of more than 45 Derek Prince offices around the world, including primary work in Australia, Canada, China, France, Germany, the Netherlands, New Zealand, Norway, Russia, South Africa, Switzerland, the United Kingdom and the United States. For current information about these and other worldwide locations, visit www.derekprince.com.

For further reading on this subject:

Marriage Covenant

Covenant is the divine key to a successful marriage and the only basis for true and lasting unity in all personal relationships. B31 *(book)*

God Is a Matchmaker

Do you want a marriage that is "made in heaven"? How can you recognize your God-appointed mate? Derek Prince reveals how this plan will guide you to your God-appointed mate. He and his wife Ruth each relate personally the story of their divinely orchestrated romance. Parents and pastors need to understand God's plan, too. B35 *(book)*

To order call 1-800-448-3261, visit us online at www.derekprince.org or write:

Derek Prince Ministries
P.O. Box 19501
Charlotte, North Carolina 28219

Books by Derek Prince

Biography
Appointment in Jerusalem
Derek Prince: A Biography
        by Stephen Mansfield
Pages from My Life's Book

Guides to the Life of Faith:
Blessing or Curse: You Can Choose
Bought with Blood
Declaring God's Word
Faith to Live By
The Grace of Yielding
How to Fast Successfully
Husbands and Fathers
Judging: When? Why? How?
Marriage Covenant
Promised Land
Rediscovering God's Church
Secrets of a Prayer Warrior
Shaping History through Prayer and Fasting
They Shall Expel Demons
Through the Psalms
War in Heaven
You Matter to God
You Shall Receive Power

Systematic Bible Exposition:
Foundations for Christian Living
Self-Study Bible Course

Write for a catalog of books, CDs and DVDs
by Derek Prince or visit us online at
WWW.DEREKPRINCE.ORG.

DEREK PRINCE MINISTRIES
P.O. BOX 19501
CHARLOTTE, NORTH CAROLINA 28219
U.S.A.

B75/0190/0213